HANDY HEALTH GUIDE

TO COLDS
FLU

Alvin and Virginia Silverstein
and Laura Silverstein Nunn

Enslow Publishers, Inc.
40 Industrial Road
Box 398
Berkeley Heights, NJ 07922
USA

http://www.enslow.com

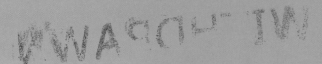

Original edition published as *Common Colds* in 2001.

Library of Congress Cataloging-in-Publication Data

Silverstein, Alvin.
Handy health guide to colds and flu / by Alvin Silverstein, Virginia Silverstein, and Laura Silverstein Nunn.
pages cm. — (Handy health guides)
Includes bibliographical references and index.
  Summary: "An overview about colds and the flu--how germs are spread, how to treat these diseases, and how to avoid becoming sick"—Provided by publisher.
  ISBN 978-0-7660-4274-2
  1. Cold (Disease)—Juvenile literature. 2. Influenza—Juvenile literature. I. Silverstein, Virginia B. II. Nunn, Laura Silverstein. III. Title.
  RF361.S556 2014
  616.2'05—dc23
                        2012041450

Future editions:
Paperback ISBN: 978-1-4644-0491-7
EPUB ISBN: 978-1-4645-1254-4
Single-User PDF ISBN: 978-1-4646-1254-1
Multi-User PDF ISBN: 978-0-7660-5886-6

Printed in the United States of America

052013 Lake Book Manufacturing, Inc., Melrose Park, IL

10 9 8 7 6 5 4 3 2 1

To Our Readers: We have done our best to make sure all Internet Addresses in this book were active and appropriate when we went to press. However, the author and the publisher have no control over and assume no liability for the material available on those Internet sites or on other Web sites they may link to. Any comments or suggestions can be sent by e-mail to comments@enslow.com or to the address on the back cover.

♻ Enslow Publishers, Inc., is committed to printing our books on recycled paper. The paper in every book contains 10% to 30% post-consumer waste (PCW). The cover board on the outside of each book contains 100% PCW. Our goal is to do our part to help young people and the environment too!

Illustration Credits: 3D4Medical/Photo Researchers, Inc., p. 9; Aaron Haupt/Photo Researchers, Inc., p. 7; AP Images/NatiHarnik, p. 34; AP Images/Ross D. Franklin, p. 13; CDC, p. 19; dedMazay/Photos.com, p. 21; Douglas Jordan, M.A./CDC, p. 40; HiBlack/Photos.com, p. 24–25; @ iStockphoto.com/Sean Locke, p. 37; James Cavallini/ Photo Researchers, Inc., p. 20; James Gathany/CDC, p. 39; Larisa Lofitskaya/Photos.com, p. 36; Shutterstock.com, pp. 1, 3, 4, 6, 11, 16, 17, 22, 23, 27, 28, 30, 31, 33, 38, 41, 42; Stockbyte/Photos.com, p. 15.

Cover Photo: Shutterstock.com

CONTENTS

Nobody likes
having a cold.
It can make you
sneeze, cough, and
have a runny nose.

1

EVERYBODY GETS SICK!

Ah-choo! You know that miserable feeling. In fact, you may be having it right now. Your nose is so stuffed up, you can't breathe. You're coughing. You feel hot and tired and just plain awful!

Sounds like you have a cold—or is it the flu? People sometimes confuse the common cold with the flu, but the two illnesses feel very different.

Doctors call colds "common colds" because they happen so often, and to so many people. In fact, chances are that you or someone you know has had a cold in the past two weeks.

Colds are not very dangerous. People usually get better in about a week, even if they don't take medicine. But colds can make you feel miserable. People miss more days of school and work because of colds than for all other diseases combined!

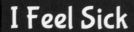
I Feel Sick

Kids get sick more often than anybody else. The average child has six to ten colds a year. As we get older, we catch fewer colds. The average adult gets two to four colds each year. You can expect to have from 50 to 100 colds in your life.

The flu is not as "common" as the common cold. Though millions of people come down with the flu each year, chances are you will get a lot more colds over your lifetime than you will get the flu.

When the flu hits you, though, its symptoms pack a powerful punch. They can make you feel so tired and achy you can't even get out of bed! Flu is also much more dangerous. It makes the body so weak that some people may wind up with another illness—and that may be life-threatening.

Why do we get sick more often when it is cold outside? In cold weather, people stay inside with the doors and windows closed and spend a lot of time with other people. This makes it easier for germs to move from one person to another. You can get a cold or the flu in the summer, too. And in tropical places, where it is hot all the time, people catch a lot of colds and flu. They get sick more often when it is rainy.

Can you tell the difference between a cold and the flu? What can you do to feel better when you get sick? Let's find out more about these illnesses.

Have you ever stayed home from school because you had a cold?

2
WHAT IS THE COMMON COLD?

The common cold is an illness that causes a stuffed-up, runny nose and a sore throat. It is caused by very tiny germs called viruses.

Viruses cannot live by themselves. They can live only inside a living animal or plant. The viruses that cause colds can live in the soft, wet lining inside a person's nose and throat. More than 200 different kinds of viruses can cause colds.

Viruses are much too small to see. In fact, you can't even see a virus with a magnifying glass or a typical microscope. Scientists need special electron microscopes to see a virus. Nobody even knew viruses existed until about a hundred years ago.

How small is a virus? Picture this: If a virus were as big as an ant, then you would be as big as the whole Earth!

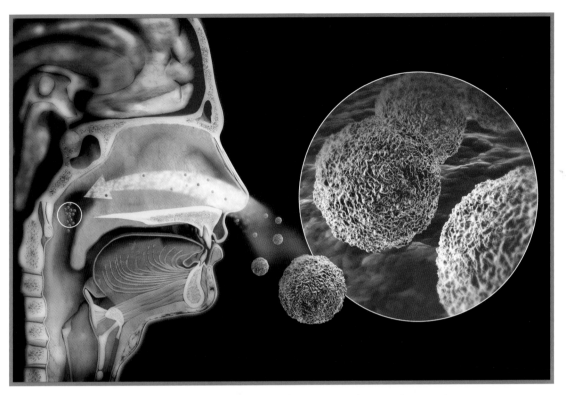

Viruses are tiny. These cold viruses have been magnified many times.

Viruses need to be inside people to make more viruses. They invade the cells in the lining of the nose and throat and turn the cells into virus-making factories. When a cell is full of viruses, it bursts open and the viruses spill out. The viruses are carried out of the body in the wet, slimy liquid that drips out. When you cough or sneeze, tiny droplets of liquid spray out and carry

Strange Ideas

Before people knew about viruses and other germs, they had some strange ideas about what caused illnesses. The ancient Greek doctor Hippocrates thought that colds were caused by waste matter in the brain. When the waste over-flowed, he said, it ran out the nose.

In the Middle Ages, people thought illnesses were caused by demons. They said that sneezing was very dangerous because a person's soul might be sneezed out, and a demon could sneak in and replace it. Saying "God bless you!" when people sneezed was a way to protect them from demons. Covering your nose and mouth when you sneezed could also protect you from demons.

viruses with them. When other people come into contact with these fluids, the viruses can invade their bodies, too. That's how viruses can spread from person to person.

By the time you feel a cold "coming on," you already have it. It can take up to two days after you are exposed to cold viruses for symptoms to develop. Colds often start off with a runny nose or a scratchy throat, then other symptoms may develop. You feel the worst after a few days and then you start feeling better until the symptoms are gone in a week or two. Bad colds are sometimes called "the flu," but the real flu is caused by a different group of viruses.

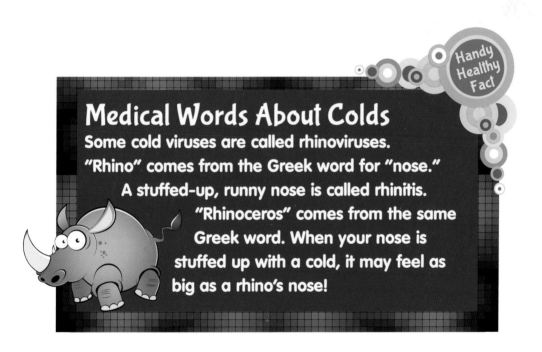

Handy Healthy Fact

Medical Words About Colds

Some cold viruses are called rhinoviruses. "Rhino" comes from the Greek word for "nose." A stuffed-up, runny nose is called rhinitis. "Rhinoceros" comes from the same Greek word. When your nose is stuffed up with a cold, it may feel as big as a rhino's nose!

3

WHAT IS THE FLU?

Flu, short for influenza, is an illness that affects the respiratory system (the breathing passages and lungs). Its main symptoms are fever, chills, cough, extreme tiredness, muscle aches, and headaches. It is caused by viruses, but they are different from the ones that cause colds.

Only two main kinds of viruses can cause influenza: type A and type B. That's far fewer than the hundreds of cold viruses around. But the flu viruses are constantly changing. The flu that is "going around" one year is usually somewhat different from the ones that were around the year before.

In 2009, an unusual influenza virus—popularly called "swine flu"—was identified. This type A flu virus had commonly been seen in pigs but somehow spread to humans. A swine flu outbreak swept across the United States during the 2009–2010 flu season, affecting millions of people. Thousands of them had to be hospitalized, and some of them died from complications. The following year, the swine flu vaccine was combined with the regular flu vaccine for added protection.

Each year's flu vaccine is different. It contains the strain of flu that specialists believe will be the one that occurs most.

I've Got the Stomach Flu

When people are throwing up, they tend to say that they have the stomach flu. But this illness is not influenza. The two conditions are both caused by viruses, but not by the same kind. The influenza virus attacks the respiratory system. Stomach viruses attack the stomach and intestines. Their main symptoms are throwing up and diarrhea. Influenza rarely involves throwing up. Actually, the so-called "stomach flu" is most likely a form of food poisoning. People can get it by drinking or eating something that contains these viruses.

Medical experts do not like to use the term "stomach flu" because they believe it confuses people about what flu really is. The stomach virus is actually a milder illness, and its symptoms usually last for only twenty-four hours or so.

In the United States, flu season usually runs from October to May. Most cases seem to occur in late December and early March.

Flu can strike anyone at any age—from babies to the elderly. But schools are a great place for viruses to run wild, so usually families with school-age children are the first to be hit by the flu bug. Unlike colds, not everybody gets the flu every year. In fact many people go for years without catching it. Those who do get the flu rarely get it more than once in a year.

Kids in school can spread the flu easily. They may rub viruses from their noses and onto their hands, and then pass the virus to friends.

Is It a Cold or the Flu?

SYMPTOM	COLD	FLU
Fever	rare	high (102 F–104 F, lasts 3–4 days)
Headache	rare	usual
Aches/pains	slight	usual, often severe
Fatigue	mild	extreme, can last up to 2–3 weeks
Runny, stuffy nose	common	sometimes
Sneezing	common	sometimes
Sore throat	common	sometimes
Cough	mild to moderate	common, can become severe

When people are hit with the flu, they usually know it. Flu symptoms tend to come on suddenly, and can really wipe a person out in no time at all. Symptoms develop between one and four days after the person has been exposed to the flu virus. That means that people can spread the disease before they even know they have it.

For most people, the flu is not a dangerous illness. The symptoms can make you feel really bad—probably worse than any cold you've had. But eventually you will get better. For some people, though, the flu can become very serious, especially for babies, pregnant women, the elderly, and people with long-term health problems such as asthma, diabetes, or heart disease. People whose body defenses have been weakened by the flu may also develop other diseases, such as pneumonia.

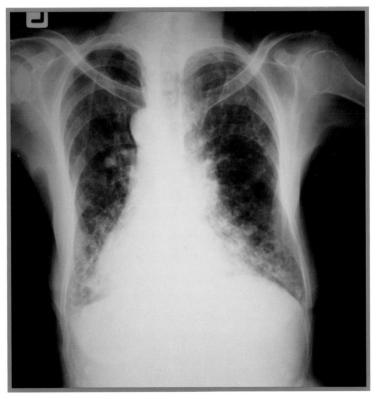

This X-ray shows shadowed areas in the lower area of this pneumonia patient's lungs.

The most serious complication of the flu is pneumonia, an infection of the lungs. Though some kinds of pneumonia are caused by viruses, the most dangerous cases of pneumonia are usually caused by bacteria. When these bacteria get past the body's defenses, they make their way into the lungs. There they can quickly multiply. Without immediate treatment, the infection can spread through the bloodstream and affect other parts of the body. So much damage may be done that the patient may die.

Every year, over 200,000 Americans wind up in the hospital from flu complications. And, each year, the flu is responsible for more than 30,000 deaths in the United States.

4

THE BODY DEFENDS ITSELF

The body has many defenses against germs. Cold or flu viruses that get into the mouth may be swept into the tonsils, where white blood cells are on patrol. Like good soldiers, the white cells surround germs and destroy them. Other viruses are swallowed. When they get down into the stomach, they are destroyed in a pool of acid.

The nose also has defenses against invading germs. Germs ride on dust particles and drops of liquid, which may be trapped by bristly hairs inside the nostrils. The germs that sneak

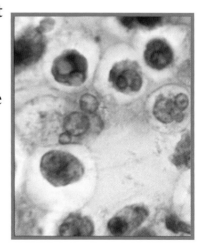

This is what your blood cells would look like if they were magnified more than 50,000 times.

past these hairs fall into the gooey fluid that covers the lining of the nose. This fluid is called mucus. The fluid flows along the lining, carrying the trapped germs toward the back of the throat. Then they may be swallowed. But the mucus does not move as fast when the air is cold and dry. Some viruses grab onto the outside of the cells and squirt some of their chemicals inside. These chemicals hold the instructions for making new cold viruses.

The cells that were invaded call for help. They use chemicals to call for the body's defenders. Some of the

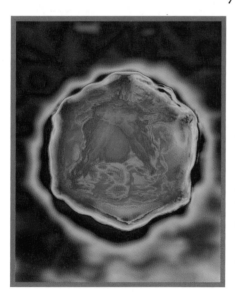

chemicals warn nearby cells about the viruses and help to protect them. Other chemicals call white blood cells. Still others make the lining leaky, so that the defending white cells can move more easily.

Viruses use the materials inside living cells to make more viruses. This rhinovirus is magnified more than 900,000 times.

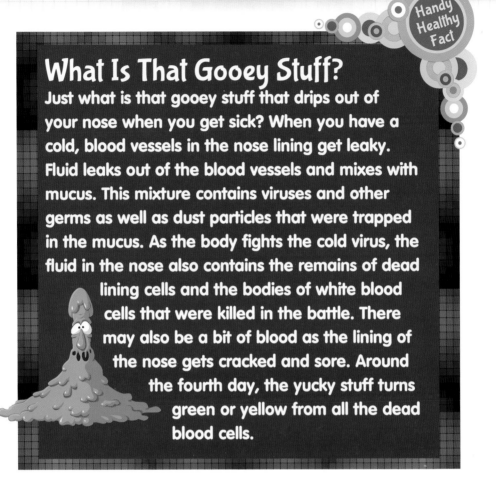

What Is That Gooey Stuff?

Just what is that gooey stuff that drips out of your nose when you get sick? When you have a cold, blood vessels in the nose lining get leaky. Fluid leaks out of the blood vessels and mixes with mucus. This mixture contains viruses and other germs as well as dust particles that were trapped in the mucus. As the body fights the cold virus, the fluid in the nose also contains the remains of dead lining cells and the bodies of white blood cells that were killed in the battle. There may also be a bit of blood as the lining of the nose gets cracked and sore. Around the fourth day, the yucky stuff turns green or yellow from all the dead blood cells.

These body defenses help to protect us against viruses, but they also cause some of the things that make us feel so miserable. The leaky lining gets swollen, and there is less room for air to flow in and out. So it gets harder to breathe. The extra mucus dribbles out, producing a runny nose. Particles that catch on the nose hairs send messages along nerves that set off a reaction

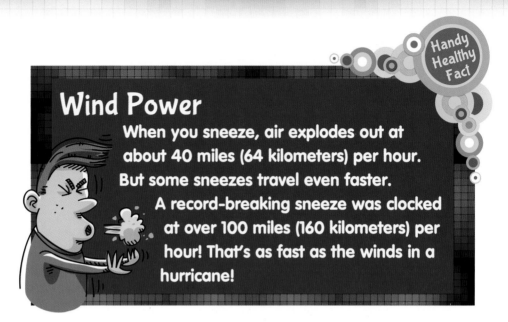

in the chest muscles and make us sneeze. Some of the extra mucus that drips down the back of the throat irritates it and makes us cough. The chemicals sent out by the damaged cells can make the brain increase the body temperature, producing fever.

Some of the white blood cells produce special chemicals called antibodies. They fit the virus, just as a key fits into a lock. Antibodies may kill germs, or they may make it easier for white blood cells to eat them. Once the body has made antibodies against the cold virus, it keeps some copies even after the cold is over. They will be ready to fight if the same kind of virus invades you again.

So, if you are protected by antibodies, why can you still catch more colds? Because there are more than 200 kinds of cold viruses, and the antibodies don't work on most of them. Older people get fewer colds than children because they have fought off more cold viruses and are protected against them. And even though there are only a couple of kinds of flu viruses, they change every year. So the antibodies won't match up from one year to the next.

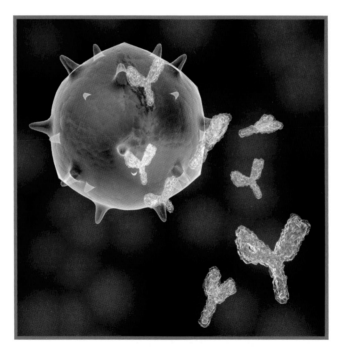

When viruses invade your body, some white blood cells produce antibodies. The antibodies (Y-shaped pink objects in this photo) attach to the viruses and help destroy them.

Diary of a Cold

Day 1
I found a new home! My old home sneezed out some viruses. They landed on her toy truck, and then her brother grabbed it. The viruses got on his hands, and then he picked his nose. Quickly my viruses dug in. Some of them settled into nice wet cells. There was plenty of food there for them. Soon the cells were making more viruses. Uh-oh! Alarms are going off. The soldiers are coming. My virus army is in for a fight!

Day 2
I think we're winning. Things are very uncomfortable, though. Some of my viruses drowned. Others were poisoned or gobbled up by those enemy soldiers. But we have them outnumbered, and we keep on making more viruses.

Day 3
It's getting hot in here, and the soldiers keep coming. We've killed a lot of them, though. My home is really complaining. He says his head hurts, and his throat hurts, and his nose is so stuffy he can hardly breathe. I wish he'd stop whining.

Day 4

It's getting wetter and wetter in here. It's hard for my viruses to find new cells before the soldiers catch them. Maybe they can escape in all that wet stuff running out of the nose.

Day 5

I'm still fighting, but things are getting very tough. The nose is still flooding.

Day 6

It's too much trouble trying to fight this. We'd better get out soon. It shouldn't be too hard to find a new home.

Day 7

Retreat! They're bringing out the big guns! They're aiming at me!

5

HOW ARE GERMS SPREAD?

When you get a cold, you might know where you got it—maybe you were playing with a friend who had been sick for a day or two. Then again, you might not have any idea where you got your cold. Maybe the store cashier passed on her cold germs when she gave you change for your purchase. But you didn't realize she had a cold.

Colds and flu are both illnesses that can spread easily from one person to another. Viruses leave the body of an infected person and get inside the body of a healthy person. How does that happen?

When you get sick, virus particles are hiding out in fluid in your eyes, nose, and throat. But how do these viruses leave your body and find a new home in

Blast From the Past

Ben Franklin slept with his windows open because he believed that fresh air prevents colds. He was right. Fresh air spreads out the virus particles in the air, making it less likely that you will breathe them in.

Handy Healthy Fact

somebody else's? Scientists say cold viruses spread in a couple of main ways. One is through the air. When you sneeze or cough—or even when you talk—tiny droplets of moisture spray out of your nose and mouth. Cold and flu viruses can ride on those tiny droplets. If you have to cough, turn your face away from your friends so they won't catch your germs.

Another way colds and flu are spread is by hands. If you rub your eyes or wipe your nose when you are sick, you can get viruses on your hands. Then if you touch somebody else's hand, you pass on some of your germs. You can also catch a cold or flu by touching an object that was recently touched by someone with a cold or flu. Viruses can survive for hours on things like doorknobs, keyboards, telephones, dishes, books, and money.

Has anybody ever told you, "Don't go outside without a jacket or you'll catch cold"? This warning is not exactly true. (Remember, colds are caused by viruses, not by the weather.) But cold weather may make it easier for you to get sick. Cold weather weakens your body's defenses. If you come into contact with cold or flu viruses, your body's white cell defenders may

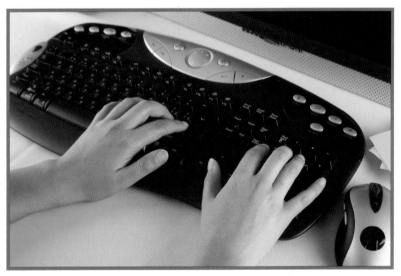

You can catch a cold by touching an object, such as a keyboard, that a sick person has touched.

Activity 1: See How Viruses Spread

Put some liquid vegetable dye in a bowl. (Use wild colors like purple, blue, or green.) Dip your fingers in the bowl to wet them with the dye. Now do some normal things, like eating a snack or bouncing a ball or drawing a picture. Every few minutes, dip your fingers in the bowl with the dye again.

After fifteen minutes, look at yourself in a mirror. How many times did you touch your face? You'll be able to tell because you will have colored spots from the vegetable dye on your skin. What else did you touch? (Hopefully you did not touch your mom's favorite white dress or the white couch!)

You probably didn't realize how often you touch your face without even thinking about it. Now can you imagine how easy it is to spread cold germs?

People catch more colds during cold weather. Wearing warm clothes can help you stay healthy.

be too weak to fight off the infection. It may also be easy to come down with a cold or flu when you are too hot, very tired, or if you have not been eating very well.

People who smoke cigarettes may have worse colds than nonsmokers. Children of parents who smoke tend to have more colds, and other health problems, too. Pollution and allergies also put a heavy load on the defenses in your nose and throat and may lead to really bad colds. In general, the more stress you have, the greater your chances are of getting sick.

Monday Blues

People get more colds on Mondays than any other day. Could it be that we do not want to go back to school or work on Monday? Well, maybe. But remember, colds take a couple of days to get started. It takes time for those viruses to multiply. So the cold that you notice on Monday was probably caught the week before, from somebody you met who had a cold.

6

TREATING COLDS AND FLU

What should you do when you get sick? Are there medications you can take to feel better? People go to doctors more for colds and flu than for any other reason. Unfortunately, doctors can't do much for someone with a cold or the flu. Of course, there are plenty of cold and flu remedies that you can buy in the supermarket or drugstore. Medications can make you feel a little better, but most of them don't fight the viruses that are making you sick.

Some people ask doctors to give them a shot of penicillin or some other antibiotic to get rid of a bad cold or the flu. Antibiotics are good drugs for diseases caused by bacteria, but they do not work on viruses. In fact, taking antibiotics too often may even be harmful,

This doctor is examining a girl who has a cold.

because they may help to breed super-germs that can't be killed by medications.

However, antiviral drugs—drugs that do kill viruses—may be used to treat the flu. These drugs help to lessen the symptoms and make them go away faster. But they have to be taken within the first two days after the symptoms appear to work well. Relenza® and Tamiflu® are common antiviral drugs.

Antibiotics can be used to treat pneumonia caused by bacteria. This infection should be treated as soon as possible. Sometimes, the infection develops so quickly that the damage to the lungs and other organs cannot be repaired even if the drugs wipe out the bacteria.

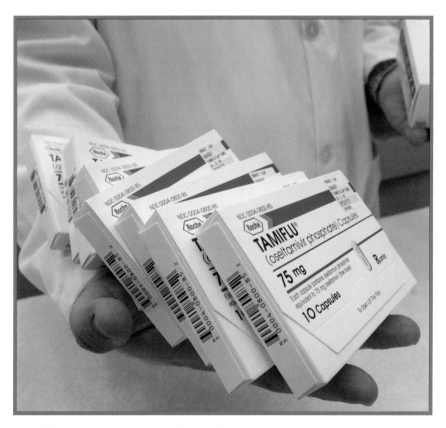

Tamiflu® is an antiviral medication used to treat the flu.

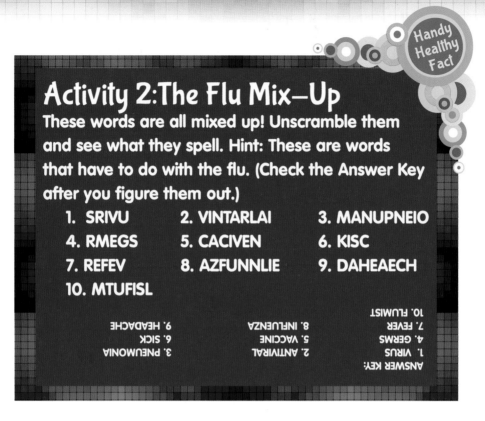

Activity 2: The Flu Mix–Up

These words are all mixed up! Unscramble them and see what they spell. Hint: These are words that have to do with the flu. (Check the Answer Key after you figure them out.)

1. SRIVU
2. VINTARLAI
3. MANUPNEIO
4. RMEGS
5. CACIVEN
6. KISC
7. REFEV
8. AZFUNNLIE
9. DAHEAECH
10. MTUFISL

ANSWER KEY:
1. VIRUS
2. ANTIVIRAL
3. PNEUMONIA
4. GERMS
5. VACCINE
6. SICK
7. FEVER
8. INFLUENZA
9. HEADACHE
10. FLUMIST

Aspirin is a popular remedy for treating illnesses like colds and flu—it helps aches and pains and headaches. But not everyone should take aspirin. In the 1970s, scientists found that children who took aspirin for a viral illness were more likely to develop Reye's syndrome, which damages the liver and nervous system. Some even died! Fortunately, Reye's syndrome is very rare. But today, doctors tell parents to give their children acetaminophen or ibuprofen instead of aspirin when they have colds and flu.

Most people treat their cold and flu symptoms at home. But some people may need to see a doctor. Colds and especially flu can be very harmful to babies, people older than seventy, pregnant women, and people who have problems with their heart and lungs. These people should call the doctor if they have:

If anyone, especially a child has a high fever for several days, he or she should see a doctor.

- symptoms that are very serious or go on for more than a week
- a fever above 102 degrees Fahrenheit (39 degrees Celsius) for more than two days
- constant coughing that prevents sleeping
- coughing that makes colored mucus for more than two days
- bad headaches, stiff neck, swollen glands, or a rash.

Colds and flu may sometimes lead to other infections such as bronchitis, tonsillitis, sinusitis, ear infections, and pneumonia. These are bacterial infections that can develop when the body is weakened by fighting cold or flu viruses. Unlike viral infections, bacterial infections can be treated with medications.

For most people with colds and flu, the only thing doctors can do is tell them to get some rest, drink plenty of fluids, keep warm, and take over-the-counter drugs to treat cold or flu symptoms. These medications can help dry up a runny nose, stop coughing, and soothe a sore throat and headache.

There are dozens of over-the-counter drugs designed to treat cold symptoms.

Some people think that taking extra vitamin C and the mineral zinc when cold symptoms first appear may prevent the cold from developing, or make it much shorter and milder.

Handy Healthy Fact

Chicken Soup! Mmm Mmm Good!

In the twelfth century, a Jewish philosopher named Maimonides said that chicken soup is good for colds. He may have been right. In 1978, Dr. Marvin Sackner of Mount Sinai Hospital in Miami Beach, Florida, found that chicken soup helped to clear the mucus from a stuffy nose much faster than other liquids.

SOUP

7

PREVENTING COLDS AND FLU

Is it possible to prevent colds? Unfortunately, there is no vaccine that can keep you from catching colds. Since there are hundreds of cold viruses, it would be really hard to protect you against all of them.

On the bright side, there is a flu vaccine. Every year, millions of people get flu shots. But they have to get a new one each year because flu viruses change each season. Medical experts use research to predict which flu viruses are going around. Then vaccines are made to protect against them.

Although there is no vaccine for the common cold, there is a vaccine for the flu.

Ouchless Flu Vaccine

Most people do not like getting shots, especially kids. But in 2003, a new kind of vaccine was approved—FluMist®. This vaccine gets sprayed in a person's nostrils. Unlike the flu shot, which contains killed viruses, FluMist is a live, but weakened vaccine. The viruses are weakened so that they do not multiply in the body. But they may cause flu symptoms in some people. Therefore, FluMist cannot be given to people with serious health problems, such as AIDS or cancer, or those with respiratory conditions, such as asthma.

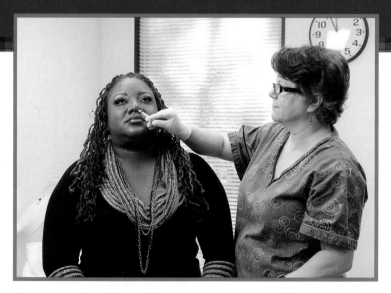

This vaccine is given to a patient by spraying it into her nostrils.

Many people do not get the flu vaccine every year. And since there is no vaccine against colds, that means lots and lots of people still get sick every year. Is there anything we can do about it?

The only sure way to keep from getting sick is to stay away from people who are sick and anything they may have touched. That's not easy. Imagine what your life would be like if you had to stay away from your sick mom or dad for a whole week! Or if they had to stay

Handy Healthy Fact

Cover Your Mouth

How many times have you heard, "Cover your mouth when you cough"? Covering your mouth when you cough or sneeze is supposed to be polite. After all, you don't want to spread your germs out into the air that other people are breathing. But coughing into your hand leaves germs there— germs that may spread to somebody else through touching. So should you cover or not cover? The best answer: Cover your mouth and then wash your hands!

away from you when you were sick! But there are things you can do to prevent colds and the flu without having to hide from sick people.

First, you need to cut down the chances for spreading colds or the flu. To keep cold or flu viruses from getting to you, try not to touch people who have these illnesses, wash your hands regularly, and always wash your hands before touching your eyes or nose. (Washing your hands won't kill the cold viruses, but it will wash them down the drain.) If you are the one

If you eat well and exercise regularly, you are less likely to catch colds.

who's sick, washing your hands often can help keep you from spreading your viruses to others.

Another important way you can keep from getting sick is to have a healthy lifestyle. You can do this by eating well, exercising regularly, getting enough rest, and practicing clean habits (washing your hands and keeping your body, clothes, food, and dishes clean). If you are healthy and strong, then your body's defenses will be strong enough to fight off invading viruses.

Some health experts believe that taking vitamin C can help keep your body strong enough to fight off diseases. Other people say you do not need to take extra vitamins because a balanced diet gives you all you need to be healthy. The problem is that you may not always eat what you should.

It's unlikely that we'll ever be able to one day wipe out colds with a cold vaccine or get everyone to get a flu shot every year. So getting sick is just a part of life. Fortunately, scientists continue to search for more effective ways to treat and possibly prevent colds and flu.

GLOSSARY

antibiotics—Medicines that kill bacteria.

antibodies—Special germ-fighting chemicals produced by white blood cells.

antiviral drugs—Medicines that kill viruses.

bronchitis—An infection of the bronchi, the hollow tubes leading from the nose and mouth down into the lungs.

electron microscope—A special kind of microscope that uses beams of electrons (particles with a negative electric charge) rather than light rays to make pictures of very tiny objects.

mucus—A gooey liquid produced by cells in the lining of the nose and breathing passages.

pneumonia—An infection of the lungs.

respiratory system—The breathing passages and lungs.

Reye's syndrome—An illness that damages the liver and respiratory system. It may develop when young people with a viral infection take aspirin.

rhinitis—A stuffed-up, runny nose.

rhinovirus—One of the main kinds of viruses that cause colds.

sinusitis—An infection of the lining of the sinuses, air-filled spaces inside the bones of the skull.

tonsillitis—An infection of the tonsils, masses of germ-fighting tissue at the back of the throat.

vaccine—A substance that stimulates the body's disease-fighting cells to produce antibodies against a particular kind of germ.

virus—The smallest kind of germ, which cannot be seen through even an ordinary microscope.

vitamin C—A nutrient chemical found in fresh fruits and vegetables that helps to keep the body's disease-fighting cells strong and active.

white blood cells—Disease-fighting cells that travel in the blood and squeeze through the tiny gaps between cells in the body tissues.

LEARN MORE

Books

Burgan, Michael. *Developing Flu Vaccines*. Chicago: Raintree, 2011.

Cobb, Vicki. *Your Body Battles a Cold*. Minneapolis, Minn.: Millbrook Press, 2009.

Grady, Denise. *Deadly Invaders: Virus Outbreaks Around the World, From Marburg Fever to Avian Flu*. Boston: Kingfisher, 2006.

Hoffmann, Gretchen. *The Flu*. Tarrytown, N. Y.: Marshall Cavendish Benchmark, 2007.

Web Sites

Nemours Foundation. "Chilling Out With Colds."
   <http://kidshealth.org/kid/ill_injure/sick/colds.
   html>

Nemours Foundation. "The Flu."
   <http://kidshealth.org/kid/h1n1_center/flu-
   basics/flu.html>

INDEX